*T*here is more to sailing than ropes and winches, cleats and bulging sails.
There are faraway places and the ever changing light, and the silence,
and a great peace at the bottom of your soul.

Ferenc Máté

SUNDAY	MONDAY	TUESDAY	WEDNESDAY	THURSDAY	FRIDAY	SATURDAY
					1 NEW YEAR'S DAY	2
3	4	5	6	7	8 ● NEW MOON	9
10	11	12	13	14 MARTIN LUTHER KING, JR.'S BIRTHDAY	15	16
17	18 MARTIN LUTHER KING, JR. DAY	19	20	21	22 ○ FULL MOON	23
24	25	26	27	28	29	30
31						

Can one ask more of life? A perfect cay protected by islands in crystal-clear waters of a hundred hues.

Jost Van Dyke, BVI   **Caribbean Sea**

JANUARY

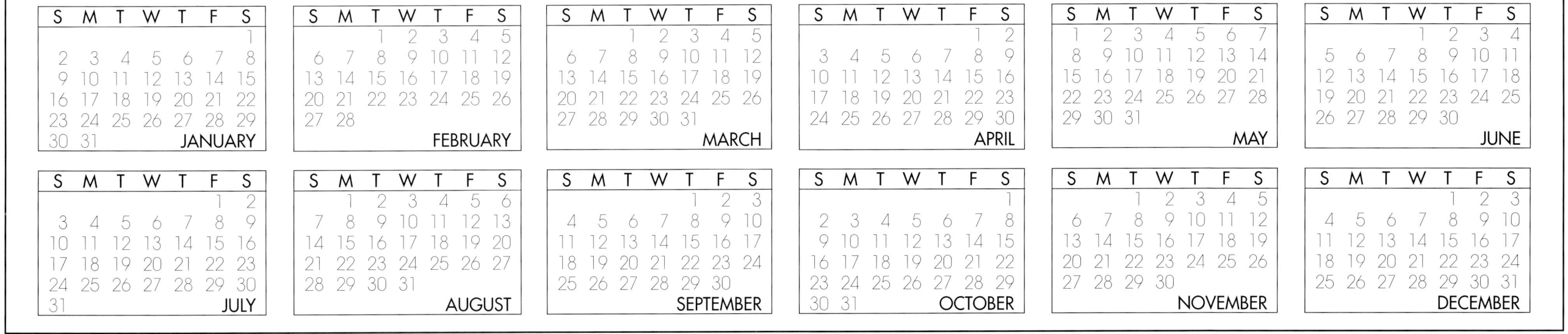

ALBATROSS PUBLISHING HOUSE

DISTRIBUTORS: USA·WW NORTON·1-800-233-4830   G.B. & EUROPE·WW NORTON·(44)20-7323-1579   CANADA·PENGUIN·1-830-668-6540   AUSTRALIA/NEW ZEALAND·JACORANDA WILEY·07-369-9755   PHOTO PRINTS: bluegreenpictures.com

SAILING BOOKS BY FERENC MÁTÉ

THE FINELY FITTED YACHT
The Boat Improvement Manual

Over 200 projects and ideas to enhance the comfort, beauty, safety and seaworthiness of your sailboat.

With chapters dedicated to the galley, chart table, engine room, cockpit, safety gear, ground tackle, sails and more, this expertly written volume is charmingly illustrated by Candace Máté. *Canadian Yachting* said, "It's brimming with clever ideas. Every boat owner should have one." While *Motorboating and Sailing* summed it up as, "Completely useful and entertaining. Don't leave port without it!"

443 pages
460 drawings & illustrations $25

SHIPSHAPE
The Art of Sailboat Maintenance

An all-inclusive step-by-step manual of sailboat maintenance. The 43 chapters cover everything from hauling out, to upkeep and repair of sailboats and their gear and equipment.

Mr. Máté worked closely with a large group of experts such as North Sails (on sail care), Barlow (on winches) and Interlux (paints and varnishes) to write what noted nautical book reviewer Roger Taylor called, "The best general maintenance book we've seen and certainly the first one we've enjoyed. Buy it. It will save you time *and* money. And you'll enjoy it too."

416 pages 460 illustrations $27.50

BEST BOATS
To Build or Buy

A selection of the best designed and built sailboats available in North America in stages from a bare hull to a finished yacht, by first class designers such as Chuck Paine, Bill Crealock and German Frers.

Lovingly written, this book is an evaluation of a wonderfully wide range of boats from the 17' Herreshoff daysailer to the 50' Santa Cruz ultra light with a vast range of cruisers and cruiser-racers in between. Mr. Máté not only points out the weakness and strength of all aspects of construction of the boats he surveyed, but also shows us what to look for when evaluating *any* sailboat.

384 pages 304 illustrations $29.95

FROM A BARE HULL
How to Build a Sailboat

A complete handbook on how to select and finish out a fiberglass hull and deck. Includes every aspect of fiberglassing, woodworking, electrical, plumbing and hardware installation.

With 100,000 copies in print, this is a nautical classic. *Sail* magazine called it, "The best guide published," while *Canadian Yachting* said, "Encyclopedic...covering every phase for the experienced and the novice...It will save buyers and builders much money, work and grief." It is the most lucid, comprehensive and—rarest of all—completely entertaining guide on boat building and finishing.

443 pages 460 illustrations $27.50

Books by Ferenc Máté are available at booksellers everywhere, or directly from W.W. Norton: 800-233-4830 http://www.wwnorton.com/

SUNDAY	MONDAY	TUESDAY	WEDNESDAY	THURSDAY	FRIDAY	SATURDAY
	1	2	3	4	5	6 ● NEW MOON
7	8	9	10	11 LINCOLN'S BIRTHDAY	12	13
14 VALENTINE'S DAY	15 PRESIDENTS' DAY	16	17 ASH WEDNESDAY	18	19	20
21 ○ FULL MOON	22 WASHINGTON'S BIRTHDAY	23	24	25	26	27
28						

Night falls on a deserted *motu*. A breath of wind stirs the lagoon, the air bursts into colors, and the sea murmurs on the reef beyond the palms.

Society Islands   **Pacific Ocean**

FEBRUARY

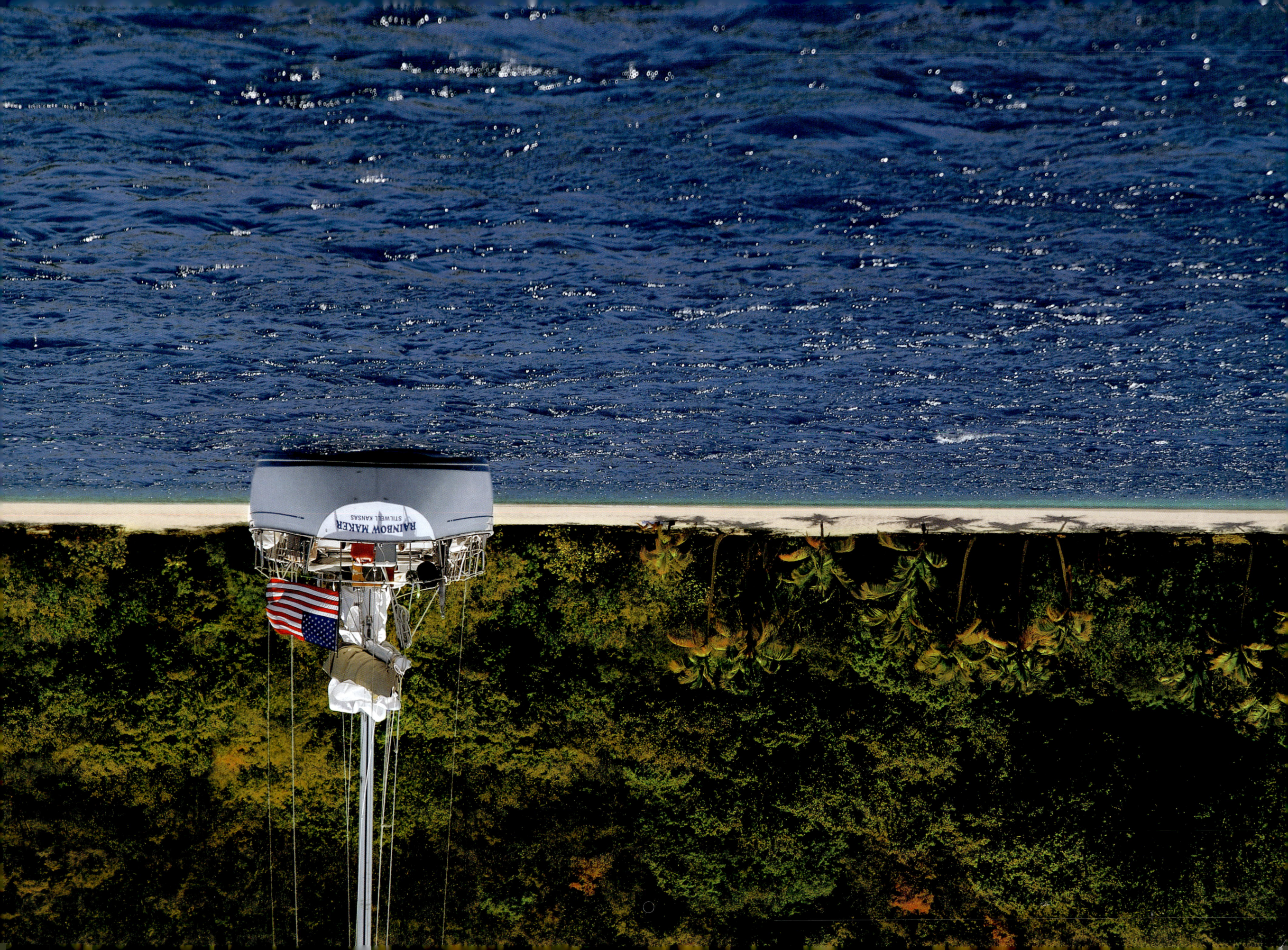

SUNDAY	MONDAY	TUESDAY	WEDNESDAY	THURSDAY	FRIDAY	SATURDAY
		1	2	3	4	5	6
7	8	9	10	11	12	13
14	15 ● NEW MOON	16	17 ST. PATRICK'S DAY	18	19	20
21	22	23	24	25	26	27
28 PALM SUNDAY	29 ○ FULL MOON	30	31			

While its crew rests under the palms, an able cruising-sloop enjoys the afternoon breeze.

St. John, Virgin Islands   **Caribbean Sea**

MARCH

SUNDAY	MONDAY	TUESDAY	WEDNESDAY	THURSDAY	FRIDAY	SATURDAY
				1	2 GOOD FRIDAY	3
4 EASTER SUNDAY	5	6	7	8	9	10
11	12	13	14 NEW MOON	15	16	17
18	19	20	21	22	23	24
25	26	27	28 FULL MOON	29	30	

S till waters of a rock-bound cove reflect verdant hills and a brooding sky.

Connemara, Ireland   **Atlantic Ocean**

APRIL

SUNDAY	MONDAY	TUESDAY	WEDNESDAY	THURSDAY	FRIDAY	SATURDAY
						1
2	3	4	5	6 ● NEW MOON	7	8
9 MOTHER'S DAY	10	11	12	13	14	15 ARMED FORCES DAY
16	17	18	19	20 ○ FULL MOON	21	22
23	24 VICTORIA DAY (CANADA)	25	26	27	28	29
30 MEMORIAL DAY	31 MEMORIAL DAY (OBSERVED)					

BAY OF BISCAY

As beautiful as small sailing ships come, a double-ender of flawless proportions plies lively waters.

La Tranche, France **Atlantic Ocean**

MAY

SUNDAY	MONDAY	TUESDAY	WEDNESDAY	THURSDAY	FRIDAY	SATURDAY
		1	2	3	4	5
6	7	8	9	10	11 ● NEW MOON	12
13	14	15	16	17	18	19 ○ FULL MOON
20 FATHER'S DAY	21	22	23 ST. JEAN (QUÉBEC)	24	25	26
27	28	29	30			

In the far north where only the melancholy howl of a timber-wolf stirs the evening calm.

Candace Cove, B.C.   **Pacific Ocean**

JUNE

SUNDAY	MONDAY	TUESDAY	WEDNESDAY	THURSDAY	FRIDAY	SATURDAY
				CANADA DAY (CANADA) 1	2	3
4 INDEPENDENCE DAY ● NEW MOON	5	6	7	8	9	10
11	12	13	14	15	16	17
18	19	20	21	22	23	24
25 ○ FULL MOON	26	27	28	29	30	31

In the serene Antarctic night, a magnificently detailed yacht revels in dreamlike light.

Sandwich Islands   The Southern Ocean

JULY

SUNDAY	MONDAY	TUESDAY	WEDNESDAY	THURSDAY	FRIDAY	SATURDAY
1	2	3	4	5	6	7
8	9 ● NEW MOON	10	11	12	13	14
15	16	17	18	19	20	21
22	23 ○ FULL MOON	24	25	26	27	28
29	30	31				

A graceful gaff-cutter ghosting to anchorage in the islands where lone lobstermen still ply the seas.

AUGUST

Downeast, Maine **Atlantic Ocean**

SUNDAY	MONDAY	TUESDAY	WEDNESDAY	THURSDAY	FRIDAY	SATURDAY
			1	2	3	4
5	6 LABOR DAY	7	8 ● NEW MOON	9	10	11
12	13	14	15	16	17	18
19	20	21	22 ○ FULL MOON	23	24	25
26	27	28	29	30		

A Galway workboat, an old kelp-drying shed and the colors of late summer on Ireland's wildest coast.

Cashel, Galway   **Atlantic Ocean**

SEPTEMBER

SUNDAY	MONDAY	TUESDAY	WEDNESDAY	THURSDAY	FRIDAY	SATURDAY
					1	2
				● NEW MOON		
3	4	5	6	7	8	9
10	11 COLUMBUS DAY (OBSERVED) THANKSGIVING DAY (CANADA)	12	13	14	15	16
17	18	19	20 LEAVE FOR ITALY	21 ○ FULL MOON	22	23
24 UNITED NATIONS DAY	25	26	27	28	29	30
31 HALLOWEEN						

Beautiful in her simplicity, a lovingly-kept schooner lies off a secluded beach.

Virgin Gorda, BVI   **Caribbean Sea**

OCTOBER

SUNDAY	MONDAY	TUESDAY	WEDNESDAY	THURSDAY	FRIDAY	SATURDAY
	1	2 ELECTION DAY	3	4 *Return from Italy*	5	6 ● NEW MOON
7	8	9	10	11 VETERANS' DAY REMEMBRANCE DAY (CANADA)	12	13
14	15	16	17	18	19	20
21 ○ FULL MOON	22	23	24	25 THANKSGIVING DAY	26	27
28	29	30				

E vening on a lagoon. A fisherman's shack on stilts catches the last light.

Raiatea, French Polynesia **Pacific Ocean**

NOVEMBER

GHOST SEA
A Novel by Ferenc Máté

IT'S JOSEPH CONRAD MEETS ELMORE LEONARD
—*Vancouver Sun*

Philosophical ... existential. A terrifying sea-story. —John Batchelor, ABC

One of the most dramatic sailing adventures of all time. —Walter Cronkite

Mystical ... like *The Heart of Darkness*. Will take you into a lost world. —*Seattle Times*

Adventure, danger, romance ... an incomparable climax ... passages that can only be decribed as poetry ... a beautifully written intellectual thriller.
—The Historical Novel Society

Ferenc Máté has reinvented the genre we haven't seen since London and Conrad: polished writing, humanism, and sheer adventure. This is the book we have waited a long time for someone to write.
—Carl Cramer, publisher, *Woodenboat Magazine*

Ghost Sea is available at all booksellers, or direct from W.W. Norton.
207 pages · $13.95 · Illustrated

Order your *Ghost Sea* at http://www.wwnorton.com/; **or** phone toll free **1-800-233-4830**; **or** send credit card information, a check or money order (U.S. dollars only) to:

W.W. Norton · 500 Fifth Ave, New York, NY 10110

Name _____
Address _____
State _____ Zip _____

_____ copies of Ghost Sea @ $13.95 each = $ _____
Shipping charges @ $2 per book = $ _____
Total = $ _____

New York and California residents please add sales tax.

 # THE SEVEN SEAS
The Sailor's Calendar   2011

THE NEW QUARTER CENTURY

One of life's great pleasures is traveling to the serene corners of the world and searching out the most picturesque settings, the fairest sailboats, the best light. To be able to share these emotions with so many of you for so many years has been a privilege. I have always held sailboats to be one of man's great creations for their perfect combination of beauty and function, for the escape and freedom they provide, and for the undisturbed world and silence they leave in their wake. I hope to bring you more reminders of what we're capable of achieving as well as the boundless beauty that we have. From the Croatian coast and the Greek Islands, to Madagascar and the Indian Ocean, from the magic of Polynesia to the brooding lochs of Scotland, I'll be photographing sunsets and dawns and the ever-changing light—and counting my blessing for a wonderful life.
Ferenc Máté

The 2011 Seven Seas Calendar is available September 1st, 2010 from booksellers, or direct from W.W. Norton.

Order your *2011 Seven Seas Calendars* at http://www.wwnorton.com/ **or** phone toll free **1-800-233-4830 or** send credit card information, a check or money order (U.S. dollars only) to:

W.W. Norton · 500 Fifth Ave, New York, NY 10110

Name _____
Address _____
State _____ Zip _____

_____ **2011 Seven Seas Calendars** @ $15.95 each = $ _____
Shipping charges @ $2 per calendar = $ _____
Total = $ _____

New York and California residents please add sales tax.

THE WORLD'S BEST SAILBOATS
Volume I

A SURVEY AND EVALUATION OF THE BEST SAILBOATS BEING BUILT TODAY: ALDENS, BALTICS, HINCKLEYS, SWANS, SHANNONS, PLUS FOURTEEN OTHERS.

This is the first nautical book which combines beauty (450 color photos by the world's leading marine photographers) and practicality. Ferenc Máté, author of *From a Bare Hull, The Finely Fitted Yacht, Best Boats to Build,* and *Shipshape,* visited the world's best boat builders from Finland to Italy, from Maine to California, and in this book describes and evaluates the sailboats of the nineteen best yards. The text is full of technical information on design and construction of available boats, while the magnificent color photos celebrate the beauty of sailboats and fine craftsmanship.

"Possibly the most beautiful sailing book ever published"—Yachting magazine

"A complete boat show between covers"—John Rousmaniere

450 full-color photographs   227 black and white illustrations   282 pages   9"x12"

Order your **World's Best Sailboats Vol. I** at http://www.wwnorton.com; **or** phone toll free **1-800-233-4830**; **or** send credit card information, a check or money order (U.S. dollars only) to:

W.W. Norton · 500 Fifth Ave, New York, NY 10110

Name _____

Address _____

State _____ Zip _____

_____ **The World's Best Sailboats Vol. I** @ $60.00 each = $_____
Shipping charges @ $2 per book   = $_____
Total   = $_____

New York and California residents please add sales tax.

THE WORLD'S BEST SAILBOATS
Volume II

A NEW SURVEY OF THE WORLD'S BEST SAILBOATS

In the classic format of *Volume I,* the even more spectacular *Volume II* (560 color photos by the world's leading nautical photographers) celebrates the giant leaps in technology and design of the last decade and a half. There are dozens of new boats of the perennial best builders such as Hinckley, Alden, Baltic and Swan, plus all the boats of seven new builders, the likes of J/Boats, Cabo Rico, Sabre and Oyster, who have over the years shown a consistency of the highest quality and most creative innovation.

Mr. Máté visited the best boatyards of Europe and North America to document this unique, first hand, scrupulous survey of the eighteen very best yards. His writing—as in his critically acclaimed *A Reasonable Life* and the international best seller *The Hills of Tuscany*—is thoughtful, engagingly direct and always entertaining. The spectacularly reproduced photographs make for a collection to be treasured.

560 full-color photographs   240 black and white illustrations   304 pages   9"x12"

Order your **World's Best Sailboats Vol. II** at http://www.wwnorton.com; **or** phone toll free **1-800-233-4830**; **or** send credit card information, a check or money order (U.S. dollars only) to:

W.W. Norton · 500 Fifth Ave, New York, NY 10110

Name _____

Address _____

State _____ Zip _____

_____ **The World's Best Sailboats Vol. II** @ $65.00 each = $_____
Shipping charges @ $2 per book   = $_____
Total   = $_____

New York and California residents please add sales tax.